D1495960

21st Century Skills Library

COOL CAREERS

FBI SPECIAL AGENT

G. S. Prentzas

Cherry Lake Publishing
Ann Arbor, Michigan

Published in the United States of America by Cherry Lake Publishing
Ann Arbor, Michigan
www.cherrylakepublishing.com

Content Adviser: Steven Aftergood, Director of the Project on Government Secrecy,
Federation of American Scientists

Library of Congress Cataloging-in-Publication Data
Prentzas, G. S.
FBI special agent / G. S. Prentzas.
     p. cm.—(Cool careers)
Includes index.
ISBN-13: 978-1-60279-304-0
ISBN-10: 1-60279-304-2
1. United States. Federal Bureau of Investigation—Vocational
guidance—Juvenile literature. I. Title. II. Series.
HV8144.F43P74 2008
363.25023'73—dc22   2008011628

Cherry Lake Publishing would like to acknowledge the work of
The Partnership for 21st Century Skills.
Please visit www.21stcenturyskills.org for more information.

TABLE OF CONTENTS

CHAPTER ONE

WHAT IS THE FBI?

FBI agents keep a very close watch on suspects when taking them to or from court.

Cameras flash wildly as a handcuffed man is escorted out of a courtroom. He has just been charged with a federal crime. Dozens of reporters want a chance to talk with the man. Local police hold the reporters and photographers back as the accused man walks through the hallway.

A few FBI special agents are escorting him to a van. They are transporting him from the courtroom to prison. He may remain in federal **custody** until his trial is finished. These agents were responsible for bringing this man to justice.

FBI stands for Federal Bureau of Investigation. The FBI is a law enforcement agency. It is the main agency of the U.S. government that investigates federal crimes. A federal crime is an act made illegal by a law passed by the U.S. Congress. Federal crimes include bank robbery, kidnapping, terrorism, and many others. FBI investigators are called special agents. These agents investigate more than 200 different kinds of federal crime. They do not investigate crimes outlawed by state and local laws. State and local police forces investigate these crimes, which include speeding, shoplifting, and murder.

The official name of the FBI's headquarters is the J. Edgar Hoover FBI Building.

By the early 1900s, improved transportation and communications boosted the U.S. economy. Moving between states became much easier. At the same time, some criminals began taking their activities across state borders. That made it harder for local and state police to catch them. The federal government needed an agency that would help capture these criminals. In 1908, Attorney General Charles Bonaparte hired investigators to work for the Department of Justice. This small group of former detectives and **Secret Service** agents did not have a name. They were just called the "special agents force." This force later was given several official names. It finally became known as the Federal Bureau of Investigation in 1935.

When the FBI first started, it handled only a few federal crimes. Most of its cases were bank robberies. The bureau's authority slowly grew over the years. In 1950, the FBI began releasing its Ten Most Wanted Fugitives list to the public. This list helped the FBI catch many dangerous criminals.

In the 1950s, Congress began passing many new laws that made certain crimes federal offenses. These new laws gave the FBI the authority to investigate some of these crimes. In 1968, Congress gave the FBI permission to conduct

About 2,185 children a day are reported missing in the United States. Some run away. Others are taken by parents who don't have legal custody. A few missing children are kidnapped by strangers. Law enforcement agencies locate almost all of these children. Four percent of missing children are never found.

The names of missing children are entered into the FBI's National Crime Information Center database. This helps law enforcement agencies throughout the country locate and identify missing children. If you were the head of a law enforcement agency, what else would you do to help find missing children?

wiretaps under certain circumstances. This helped the bureau investigate and bring down **organized crime** groups. The Patriot Act of 2001 expanded the FBI's role in preventing terrorism.

Today, the FBI employs more than 30,000 people. It has more than 12,000 special agents. The bureau's headquarters are located in Washington, D.C. The FBI also has more than 400 offices, which are located in smaller U.S. cities and in foreign countries. The FBI is one of the most respected law enforcement agencies in the world.

CHAPTER TWO

WORKING FOR THE FBI

Working as an FBI special agent can be dangerous. Bulletproof vests protect agents from gunfire.

The FBI's job is to investigate violations of more than 200 federal criminal laws. It's a big job. Any time there is a bank robbery or a kidnapping, local police call in the FBI. The FBI protects the United States from espionage, or spying by foreign governments. The bureau investigates all violations of national security.

Since 2001, the FBI has helped protect the United States from **domestic** and international terrorism.

The FBI also helps other police agencies. Local, state, federal, and international law enforcement agencies benefit from the bureau's resources. The FBI provides technical assistance, such as fingerprint identifications and laboratory testing. It also offers other agencies advanced law enforcement training and technology training.

FBI special agents have many responsibilities. Agents spend most of their time "in the field" investigating crimes. Field investigations involve viewing crime scenes and interviewing

FBI agents rely on scientists to help analyze evidence.

witnesses. During an investigation, agents talk to people who have information about the crime or the suspects. They research and gather evidence on the suspected criminals. Agents inspect business and public records. They work with crime lab technicians and other FBI experts. They may follow and watch suspects. Sometimes they even go **undercover**. The agent's goal is to find out who is responsible for the crime.

Special agents usually work by themselves. For some cases, they work in pairs. For most cases, an FBI agent investigates the crime and writes a report. Based on the agent's report, other government agencies make the actual arrest. These agencies may invite the special agent involved with the case to be present at the suspect's arrest. Many times, the agent has already moved on to his or her next case.

Special agents investigate many different types of crime. They investigate major thefts, such as bank robberies, stolen art, and stolen jewelry. They also handle cases involving kidnapping, major crimes on Native American reservations, and crimes committed aboard airplanes and cruise ships. They investigate **identity theft** cases and white-collar crimes. White-collar crimes are committed

Sometimes FBI agents dress in everyday clothes on the job. They may pretend to be someone else to get information.

by business and government professionals. These crimes usually involve **fraud**. White-collar crimes include corporate fraud, insurance fraud, and telemarketing fraud.

Special agents also investigate three other special types of crime. Cybercrimes are crimes in which computers or the Internet play a key role in the illegal activity. **Hacking** and copyright violations are two common types of cybercrime. Organized crime activities include the illegal sale of guns and drugs, sports bribery, and murder. Civil rights crimes include **hate crimes** and certain criminal acts committed by government officials.

A special agent's job is difficult, exciting, and rewarding. Agents often work long hours. They spend a lot of time away from their offices and families. They always carry mobile phones and pagers. They are required to be available every hour of every day. The job is never boring!

CHAPTER THREE

BECOMING AN FBI SPECIAL AGENT

FBI representatives visit college campuses to find new agents.

Working as an FBI special agent is challenging and interesting. It's also a rewarding way to serve your country. But becoming an FBI special agent is not easy. The FBI is very selective. Tens of thousands of people apply for special agent jobs each year. Only several hundred are hired. The bureau has certain age, education, and physical fitness requirements.

Candidates for the job of special agent go through a long, hard application process. They take written tests. They are interviewed several times. The bureau conducts a thorough background check of each candidate. If you apply for a job as an FBI special agent, you must allow the FBI to investigate your background. They will interview you, your friends, your teachers, and others. They will check your school and work records.

To be a special agent candidate, you must meet several basic requirements. You must be a U.S. citizen. You must be between the ages of 23 and 36. You must have a four-year college degree. You must be able to pass a tough physical fitness test. You must pass a medical examination, which includes vision and hearing tests. Male candidates must be registered with the **Selective Service System**.

FBI special agents must be in good shape. A timed run is part of candidate fitness testing.

You must have a driver's license. You must pass a drug-screening test.

Several things will disqualify you from becoming a special agent. You cannot have been convicted of a **felony**

Life & Career Skills

What can you do to become an outstanding special agent candidate? You should take college courses that improve your reasoning and critical-thinking skills. Choose an academic or employment field that you're interested in, such as accounting or law enforcement. In your academic work and at your jobs, show that you are a person with good judgment and maturity. Learn a foreign language. Arabic, Chinese, Farsi, Russian, Spanish, and Vietnamese are among the languages most needed by the FBI. Keep yourself in good physical shape. Don't take drugs. All of these skills and qualities will help in whatever career you choose.

in the past. You cannot have used illegal drugs frequently in the past or at any time in the last 3 to 10 years before your application. You cannot fail a polygraph (lie detector) test.

FBI special agents come from many different academic and employment fields. You may want to choose a college major or develop specific job skills that the FBI needs. For new special agents, the FBI has five different entrance programs. Here are the programs and the education or training needed:

1. Law Program: You must have a law degree from an accredited law school.

2. Accounting Program: You must have a college degree in business

During training, agents learn how to arrest and handcuff suspects.

or accounting. You must pass the Certified Public Accountant exam.

3. Language: You must have a college degree, plus proven ability in a language.

4. Information Technology: You must have a degree in computer science, information technology, or electrical engineering. Or you must be a certified information technology professional.

5. Diversified: You must have a college degree, plus three years of work experience. Or you must have an advanced degree, plus two years of work experience.

Learning & Innovation Skills

Imagine that you're an FBI special agent. Your supervisor sends you a complaint filed by a resident of a large city. He claims that a city police officer falsely arrested him for a theft. He insists that the officer arrested him out of revenge. He had been in a fight with the officer's nephew two weeks earlier. It's a federal crime for police officers to go beyond the limits of their authority. Courts have held that police officers must have a good reason for making an arrest.

If you were investigating the man's claims, what type of evidence would you look for? Who would you interview?

At the end of the application process, the FBI will inform you of their hiring decision. If they accept you as a special agent trainee, you will spend 18 weeks training at the FBI Academy. The FBI Academy is located in Quantico, Virginia. There you'll learn the basic skills you will need to be a special agent. You will take courses on how to interview witnesses, question suspects, and evaluate evidence. You will learn how to defend yourself and others. This includes how to use firearms. The special agent program also involves physical training. You will have to be ready to do a lot of sit-ups, push-ups, and running!

Instructors teach agents how to safely operate firearms.

If you finish the training program, you will be sworn in as a special agent. During their first two years on the job, new agents must show that they can use the basic skills learned at Quantico. They also receive on-the-job training from more experienced special agents. New agents must agree to serve for three years. Which field office an agent

Agents must have good communication skills. At times,
they may need to speak with the media.

is assigned to depends on the FBI's needs. Agents are often

required to relocate to other offices. Many agents move

several times during their careers.

Unlike employees in many other careers, FBI agents

stay at their jobs for many years. Not counting those

who retire, only 4 percent of all special agents quit the FBI each year. Agents must retire at age 57 or after 20 years in the field. Most agents go to work elsewhere after their retirement. Using the skills they learned as FBI agents, they usually enter a field in their area of expertise. Many stay in law enforcement. They work for other federal agencies, such as the Bureau of Alcohol, Tobacco, Firearms and Explosives or the Central Intelligence Agency. Some work for state or local police forces. Other agents find a variety of different jobs. Some work at private laboratories, teach, or become attorneys or private investigators.

CHAPTER FOUR

THE FUTURE OF THE SPECIAL AGENT

Acts of terrorism involving germs may increase in the future. FBI agents need to be prepared to investigate these crimes.

The duties of an FBI special agent have always changed over time. That's because the nature of crime has changed. Agents in the early 1900s mostly handled bank robberies and financial crimes. Today, agents investigate many other types of crimes. Agents in the future will face new and different challenges.

Since the 1990s, advances in transportation and technology have changed the way countries connect with one another. This trend, known as **globalization**, will continue to increase the flow of information and people between countries. It will also allow criminals to move more easily around the world. The FBI expects increased threats in the future from international organized crime and terrorist groups.

In the future, more of the FBI's work will take place abroad. The bureau will have a greater need for special agents with foreign language skills. The rapid advance of technology will also have an impact on FBI investigations. The FBI will need special agents who know a lot about using computers.

The FBI forecasts that the future will bring an increase in the number and types of crimes that it investigates. Since 2001, the FBI has focused many of its resources on

Life & Career Skills

The FBI offers many other career opportunities. The bureau employs workers who help special agents do their jobs. Scientists in the FBI crime labs analyze evidence. FBI computer specialists provide information technology assistance. Intelligence analysts examine documents and reports related to spying and terrorism cases. Language specialists translate documents and help conduct witness interviews. Solving crimes often requires many people with different skills working together. Visit www.FBIJobs.gov to learn more about all types of careers in the FBI.

preventing terrorism. The bureau expects that terrorist groups will cooperate with each other more in the future. That means the raw materials and know-how to build nuclear and biological weapons may become easier to obtain.

Cybercrimes will also increase in the future. Many traditional crimes, such as fraud, will continue to shift to the Internet. This will make it even more difficult for agents to catch criminals. As the nation's economy becomes more dependent on computer networks, illegal use of public and private networks will rise.

The FBI forecasts that public corruption cases will increase in the

*Computer skills are becoming even more important
for FBI agents as cybercrimes increase.*

future. Government spending is expected to increase, which means that there will be more opportunities for government officials to commit fraud and other crimes. The FBI also expects an increase in illegal drug sales and white-collar crimes. One type of white-collar crime that the bureau expects to grow is health care fraud. The overall population of the United States is aging. By 2030, almost one out of every five Americans will be 65 years or older. Private and public health care spending will increase, which will lead to more cases of health care fraud.

A career as a special agent can be exciting, challenging, and rewarding. It requires a lot of education, good physical fitness, and a desire to serve your country. If you think you can live up to the FBI's motto—Fidelity, Bravery, and Integrity—you should learn more about becoming an FBI special agent.

SOME FAMOUS FBI AGENTS

Candace DeLong (1950–) worked as an FBI agent for 20 years. She became a field profiler, collecting evidence to understand a criminal's behavior and character.

J. Edgar Hoover (1895–1972) served as FBI director for 48 years (1924–1972). Under his direction, the FBI's authority and importance grew.

John O'Neill (1952–2001) served as special agent in charge of terrorism investigations. He helped capture Ramzi Yousef, who was convicted of the 1993 World Trade Center bombing. He also investigated the bombings of U.S. embassies in Kenya and Tanzania (1998) and the attack on the USS *Cole* (2000).

Joe Pistone (1939–) worked as an undercover agent in the 1970s. Posing as a jewel thief named Donnie Brasco, he became a member of an organized crime group, the Bonnano family. He gathered evidence and testimony against family members, leading to 120 convictions.

Melvin Purvis (1903–1960) gained fame during the 1930s for bringing several violent criminals to justice. He led teams of agents who caught well-known outlaws John Dillinger and Charles Arthur "Pretty Boy" Floyd. Both Dillinger and Floyd were killed in shoot-outs with bureau agents.

Glossary

custody (KUHSS-tuh-dee) control of a suspect by a law enforcement authority

domestic (duh-MESS-tik) originating within one's own country

felony (FEL-uh-nee) a major crime, such as robbery or murder

fraud (FRAWD) the intentional use of dishonesty to gain money or property illegally

globalization (glohb-uhl-uh-ZAY-shuhn) the growth of international economic activity, which includes increased movement of goods, money, and people between countries

hacking (HAK-ing) illegally accessing someone else's computer system to destroy, disrupt, or commit a crime

hate crimes (HATE KRIMEZ) crimes against a person or property motivated by the lawbreaker's prejudice against a race, religion, or other attribute

identity theft (eye-DEN-ti-tee THEFT) when someone uses another person's personal information, such as their name or credit card number, to commit a crime

organized crime (or-guh-nized KRIME) crimes committed by a large group of people who work together to profit from illegal activity

Secret Service (SEE-krit SUR-viss) a federal law enforcement agency that protects national and visiting government leaders and investigates some federal crimes

Selective Service System (si-LEK-tiv SUR-viss SIS-tuhm) a federal government program in which young men provide contact information in case they are needed in the military in time of war

undercover (uhn-dur-KUHV-ur) posing as a criminal or other person to get information about a suspect or gather evidence about a crime

wiretaps (WIRE-taps) devices that allow law enforcement agents to gather information by listening in on telephone and other conversations

For More Information

Books

Baker, David. *CIA & FBI*. Vero Beach, FL: Rourke Publishing, 2006.

Cunningham, Kevin. *J. Edgar Hoover: Controversial FBI Director*. Minneapolis: Compass Point Books, 2006.

Hamilton, John. *The FBI*. Edina, MN: ABDO Publishing, 2007.

Web Sites

Federal Bureau of Investigation—Kids' Page
www.fbi.gov/fbikids.htm
Find out more about the FBI through games, tips, and stories

Federal Bureau of Investigation—Careers
www.fbijobs.gov
Learn more about working for the FBI

INDEX

ABOUT THE AUTHOR

G. S. Prentzas has written more than a dozen books for young readers. He works as an editor and writer. He lives in New York state.